Beautiful
Los Angeles

Beautiful
Los Angeles

Text by William Curran

Library of Congress Cataloging in Publication Data
Curran, William, 1921-
  Beautiful Los Angeles
    1. Los Angeles—Description—Views.
I. Title.
F869.L843C87   917.94'94   79-12045
ISBN 0-89802-056-5
ISBN 0-89802-055-7 (paperback)

First Printing July 1979

Published by Beautiful America Publishing Company
P.O. Box 608, Beaverton, Oregon 97005
Robert D. Shangle, Publisher

PHOTO CREDITS

ROY BISHOP—*page 9; page 10, below; page 11; page 14; page 15; pages 16-17; page 18, below; page 19; page 20; page 21; page 22; page 23, below; page 24; page 25; pages 28-29; pages 32-33; page 36, below; page 37; page 40, below; page 42; page 43, below; pages 44-45; page 46; page 47, above; pages 48-49; page 50, below; page 51; page 53; page 54; page 55, below; page 56; page 57; page 60; page 61, above; pages 64-65; page 68; page 69; page 72.*

JOHN HILL—*pages 12-13; page 36, above; page 40, above; page 41; page 47, below; page 52; page 61, below.*

ROBERT D. SHANGLE—*page 10, above; page 18, above; page 23, above; page 43 above; page 50, above; page 55, above.*

Enlarged Prints

Most of the photography in this book
is available for photographic enlargements.
Send self-addressed, stamped envelope
for information.
Beautiful America Publishing
Company
P.O. Box 608
Beaverton, Oregon 97005

CONTENTS

Beautiful America Publishing Company

The nation's foremost publisher of quality color photography

CURRENT BOOKS

Alaska, Arizona, British Columbia, California, California Vol. II, California Coast, California Desert, California Missions, Colorado, Florida, Georgia, Hawaii, Los Angeles, Idaho, Illinois, Maryland, Michigan, Michigan Vol. II, Minnesota, Montana, Montana Vol. II, Mt. Hood (Oregon), New York, New Mexico, Northern California, Northern California Vol. II, North Idaho, Oregon, Oregon Vol. II, Oregon Coast, Oregon Mountains, Portland, Pennsylvania, San Diego, San Francisco, Texas, Utah, Washington, Washington Vol. II, Washington, D.C., Wisconsin, Yosemite National Park.

FORTHCOMING BOOKS

California Mountains, Indiana, Kentucky, Las Vegas, Massachusetts, Mississippi, Missouri, Nevada, New Jersey, North Carolina, Oklahoma, Ozarks, Rocky Mountains, San Juan Islands, Seattle, South Carolina, Tennessee, Vermont, Wyoming.

LARGE FORMAT, HARDBOUND BOOKS

Beautiful America, Beauty of California, Glory of Nature's Form, Lewis & Clark Country, Western Impressions.

Send $1.00 for complete catalog
Beautiful America Publishing Company
Robert D. Shangle, Publisher
Post Office Box 608
Beaverton, Oregon 97005

INTRODUCTION

When I was in the seventh grade, back before the Second World War, a classmate came to school one morning and announced smugly that she was moving to Los Angeles. The scene was a barren schoolyard in a large East Coast city, notorious for its bad weather. The season was March—cold, gray, gusty and damp. Her words shriveled me with envy. Every cliche' of travel brochure prose flashed in my brain: laden orange trees against a background of snow-capped mountains; broad, palm-lined boulevards and white mansions with red tiled roofs; an ocean of deepest blue gently lapping at endless miles of golden strand and rocky bluffs; long-legged blonde bathing beauties, more numerous than California poppies; movie cowboys driving Duesenbergs upholstered in black-and-white cowhide; and thousands of smiling, handsome tanned, healthy, oil-rich, informally-dressed young Californians with one hand on the wheel of a white convertible and an arm around a Rose Bowl princess. And, indelibly, every vision was bathed in beneficent sunshine. With heartbreaking swiftness, the girl was gone from her desk, whisked by the 20th Century Limited and Santa Fe Chief to a land that had banished galoshes from its hall closets. How I hated her.

Not very many years later, I, too, got to stand in that sunshine. It was in the patio of the still new Union Station on an autumn morning. The sky was bluer than any post card could duplicate, the air warm and fragrant. Palms, pepper trees and even a few olive trees seemed at once familiar but unreal. In defiance of the calendar, bright flowers bloomed around the station. Further downtown, along Spring, Main and Broadway, Los Angelenos walked the street unhurried and with heads up. Many were remarkably pretty girls. Seen from my hotel window, the Santa Monica Mountains created a spectacular natural boundary to the west and in between lay a broad city of boulevards, exotic greenery and low white buildings, almost dazzling in the sunshine. Whether that sight truly matched my preconceptions, I can't remember. I do remember that I was not disappointed, not then, nor have I been since. Los Angeles was like no other place I had ever seen and it has never been exactly the same on any two visits. It's a metaphor for adventure.

Writers sometimes complain that any commentary on the city risks being outdated before it comes off the press. One has suggested that guidebooks be done on ticker tape. Assuredly, things do change fast. It's a pace of urban development that the world has never witnessed before, hence the designations "ultimate city," "city of the future," "prototype of the supercity." These terms reinforce what urbanologists have been telling us: look at Los Angeles and you have looked into the future.

In a tired nightclub joke born in the 1920s, Los Angeles is described as "six suburbs in search of a city." With time and retelling, the number of suburbs increases to 14, then 24. It has gone as high as 80. The old joke implicitly acknowledges that the Los Angeles Basin constitutes something new in urban life, a giant mosaic of communities joined in a loose regional federation of common concerns. Social historian Spencer Crump, a native son of Long Beach, calls it the City of Southern California. That may prove in the long run to be the truest and most convenient name.

In its particulars the political map of the Basin is complex. Collectors of curious facts delight in recounting the way the City of Los Angeles entirely surrounds many other cities and these, in turn, may surround even smaller cities or postage-stamp portions of Los Angeles County, like a parody of the Chinese Boxes. But most observers are willing to let "Los Angeles," or "L.A.," stand for the contiguous area that touches the five counties of Los Angeles, Orange, Riverside, San Bernadino and Ventura. This L.A. is comprised of three concentric zones: the City of Los Angeles, the County of Los Angeles, and the Los Angeles Basin.

Inevitably, Los Angeles provokes superlatives. To begin with, it's big—464 square miles for the City, 4,069 for the County. And that leaves out the urban areas of the other four counties. If Los Angeles County alone were a separate state, it would be larger than Rhode Island and Delaware combined. In addition to L.A. itself, the County shelters some 70 cities and towns, and the entire Basin contains about 180, although figures vary with the source. More than three million persons live in the City, about seven million in the County and perhaps as many as ten million in the Basin.

Although it is one of the nation's greatest manufacturing centers, specializing in aerospace technology, clothing, and motion pictures, Los Angeles County is still sufficiently rural to rank 20th nationally in agriculture. Until recently, it ranked first. Within one hundred miles of City Hall can be found every kind of terrain and climate on earth except perhaps Arctic tundra, a shortcoming which has caused no hardship. Elevations range from sea level to over five thousand feet within the City, up to ten thousand in the County. It is possible to ski in the morning and surf the same afternoon, if a person is so inclined. Los Angelenos own more motor vehicles, more private swimming pools, more household pets, more Frisbees, more electric pencil sharpeners and more anything-else-you-want-to-name per capita than do any urban dwellers in the world.

Consistent with its zeal for futurity, Los Angeles has been a proving ground for new customs which have influenced behavior around the world. Angelenos have pioneered the development of cafeterias, supermarkets, freeways, motels, drive-in services, seven-day-a-week and 24 hour retailing, flex time for industrial workers and much more. Significantly, all concern a fast-paced, highly mobile society.

Perhaps because Los Angeles has acted as the cutting edge of a new age, it has been the target of a record volume of abuse, so much that W.W. Robinson has anthologized the attacks in his book, *What They Say About the Angels*. Some criticism has been of the kidding kind—from Fred Allen, Herb Caen, Woody Allen and others. The bulk, however, has been passionately hostile. Inexplicably, the most common charge is that Los Angeles "lacks culture." These detractors look right past the Music Center, the County Art Museum, the Huntington Library, more than 25 theaters, and a public library system that circulates more books than does any other in the world, to cite only the most obvious. Los Angeles has also been pilloried for the number and diversity of its religious and philosophical groups, its innovative cuisine, its hours of business, its street-corner orators, its individualistic modes of dress and a dozen other manifestations of free expression. But in the final analysis, it is Angelenos who play tennis in February while their critics are blowing on frost-nipped fingers.

Newcomers keep arriving daily. In less than a century, Los Angeles has experienced the most rapid and massive growth in population in the history of human settlement, from a scant 11,000 in 1880 to more than three million today. The 1980 census is almost certain to confirm it as the country's second largest city.

What is the magic that continues to draw people from 49 other states and uncounted foreign countries? An oft-quoted bit of enthusiasm from Boston native Jack Lemmon may suggest an answer.

"One of the first mornings I was here . . . driving into town on Sunset, I looked up and there were the mountains on a clear morning with snow on top and I was . . . in a T-shirt and the ocean was behind me."

Many people have commented on the juxtaposition of snowy mountains with semi-tropical seashore: it's one of the first things a visitor notices, the first coherent impression L.A. makes. But it doesn't seem to be the landscape they're reflecting on as much as the possibilities it suggests, the diversity that continues to defy summing

(Preceding page) Los Angeles City Hall, still an impressive structure, was for many years the tallest building in Los Angeles. In the foreground is the Triforium, a sculpture which features lights and music coordinated electronically.

(Left) Hibiscus enjoy the mild Los Angeles climate, producing extravagant displays of color.

(Below) The Mark Taper Forum faces a reflecting pool in the L.A. Civic Center.

(Opposite) Strollers and sun-worshippers enjoy this Beverly Hills park, across from the Beverly Hills Hotel.

(Following pages) Not far from the city, a desert ambiance preveils. This Joshua Tree was photographed near Baker.

(Third following page) Fishermen's Village, at Marina del Rey, offers a perfect environment for shopping and sightseeing.

(Third preceding page, above) The Queen Mary, *a retired ocean liner, now rests at anchor in Long Beach Harbor, housing shops and a hotel.*

(Third preceding page, below) The architecture of Pasadena's Ambassador Auditorium makes good use of fountains and reflecting pools.

(Preceding pages) From Griffith Park Observatory the city spreads as far as the eye can see.

(Left) Roses bloom in Los Angeles gardens.

(Below) Mission San Gabriel preserves a touch of the ambiance of Old California under Spanish rule.

(Opposite) This stretch of Wilshire Boulevard is called the ''Miracle Mile.''

(Following page) Spring rains bring bright floral displays to the deserts outside of Los Angeles.

(Second following page, above) The gentle headlands of the Southern California coastline form many secluded coves like this one.

(Second following page, below) Flags of many nations are displayed on the Flag Mall in front of L.A. Hall.

(Opposite) The Ferndell in Griffith Park shows the variety of plant life adaptable to the Southern California climate.

(Right) Pasadena, with its annual Rose Parade, has a particular affection for the rose.

(Below) The play of lights and the sound of falling water in the Convention Center provides a pleasant oasis in downtown Los Angeles.

(Following page, above) Night falls at Aliso Beach.

(Following page, below) A look at Marina del Rey will give an idea about the popularity of pleasure boating in Southern California.

up. Yes, it *is* possible to ski and surf on the same day, if you hustle; and the lesson Los Angeles learns from its geography seems to be applied in the whole attitude of the place. It's possible to do anything if you hustle, and that is what Los Angeles is about.

So perhaps it's not mere chance that the city lacks a unifying landmark, an Eiffel Tower, a Washington Monument, or a Tower Bridge that says to the world "This is Los Angeles." Los Angeles is not characterized by buildings, though the city has a lot of striking ones; nor other human artifacts, though it has at least one of anything you could name. Even L.A. freeways look just about like other freeways the world over, though that's probably backwards: freeways the world over are patterned after L.A. freeways. Either way, that's not the point: intangibles characterize Los Angeles. The energy, the pace, the possibilities . . . the style and the hustle . . . are the magic of Los Angeles.

The most appropriate landmark, if Angelenos were moved to create one, would be a giant statue of Heraclitus on Mt. Hollywood, overlooking the city which so perfectly illustrates the natural law which he put into words: "All is flux. Nothing remains the same."

(Preceding page) Carefully manicured trees and lawns grace the entry plaza of Beverly Hills City Hall.

Downtown

Whenever a comedian of 25 years ago—often a New Yorker on tour—complained slyly that he got lost in Pershing Square trying to find his way downtown, he was asking, "Where are your skyscrapers?" as if to suggest that without them you couldn't have a city. Until the 1960s there was a legal height limit on Los Angeles buildings as a precaution against earthquakes and to ensure that sunlight and air would reach the streets. Only City Hall was permitted to exceed the 150-foot limit. It helped give the city a uniquely spacious look. The aura of space is still there, but like many major cities of the world, Los Angeles has grown its crop of skyscrapers. Today, United California Bank's 62 stories dwarf City Hall.

Among the new skyscrapers the modestly tall Occidental Center on 12th Street has a particular charm. Its garden court is one of the most pleasant spots in Central City and the view from its observation deck cannot be improved upon. The 52-story ARCO Towers, whose expanse of dark glass looks down the venerable Bunker Hill section may best symbolize the renaissance that has seized downtown. Not very many years ago single families occupied handsome Victorian mansions on Bunker Hill. Now the Atlantic Richfield complex with its offices, shops, restaurants and other services administers to more persons in a day than lived in the city when the old mansions were built.

Before the age of jet aircraft most visitors arrived by train at Union Station in the center of town. It was a good place to start, at the Old Plaza, where this supercity had its beginnings. The original colonists of Spanish Governor de Neve were told in 1781 that they had arrived at El Pueblo de Neuestra Senora la Reina de Los Angeles de Porciuncula. Despite its sonority, this was a name that begged to be shortened. It soon shrank to the more manageable "Los Angeles," then to the admirably simple "L.A." Having survived a period of neglect, the Plaza today shows that it has shared in the renaissance of downtown. It has been restored as an historic landmark and serves as a tasteful oasis in the center of a modern city. Narrow old Olvera Street with its many puestos and shops adds an appropriate Mexican flavor. Among the old buildings preserved are the Mission Church, the Pico House (finest hotel of its day), the Old Firehouse and the Merced Theater.

Perhaps nothing could better convey the feeling of L.A.'s enthusiastic push toward the future than the fact that the new Civic Center is just a short walk from the site of the pueblo. Presently covering six blocks, the Civic Center is the largest

(Left) Fond of fountains and flowers, Angelenos managed to produce this spectacular combination of both at the Rose Garden Exposition Park on U.S.C. campus.

complex of public buildings west of Washington D.C. At the east end of the landscaped mall is City Hall, still a handsome building at age 50. On the west end, facing City Hall is the many-layered Water and Power Building. In a pagan age, W & P, as it is sometimes called, might have been a temple to the principal god of a city that lies on an arid plain. Almost all the city's water and power have to be imported from ''beyond tribal boundaries.'' The suggestion of a sanctuary is strengthened by the fact that the building is always lighted. It's a favorite nighttime landmark of Angelenos. A welcome surprise in this governmental complex is the Music Center, standing in the protective shadow of Water and Power. Los Angeles has put the Dorothy Chandler Pavilion, home of the Philharmonic, the Mark Taper Forum and the Ahmanson Theater—all built with private funds—right in the center of the most serious business of life—government. Surely this choice says something about the feeling of Los Angeles for the arts.

Downtown is the best place to experience the rich, pluralistic character of the population. The old barrio—the term has little meaning now in a city more than a quarter Hispanic—used to run along Alameda Street. Now much of the east side, across the Los Angeles River, is part of the Mexican-American community. The many Mexican shops, restaurants, and signs in Spanish mark this colorful bilingual area. Along North Broadway not far from Dodger Stadium is the city's Chinatown, the third location of the city's long established Chinese-American community. The second Chinatown was razed to make way for Union Station. Although not as large as San Francisco's Chinatown, it nonetheless introduces a charming oriental flavor to the city's center. Little Tokyo—between First and Third east of Alameda Street—is the original Japanese community in the city, though Japanese-Americans now live in all parts of Los Angeles. A good place to observe the city's diverse population close up and to hear many foreign languages is the Grand Central Public Market on Broadway. Its more than 150 shops and stalls offer a seemingly endless variety of foods, many imported.

There are things missing from downtown that we might wish had not gone. The old mansions on Bunker Hill offered a quiet contrast to what was even 30 years ago a busy metropolitan center. However, the serious student of Victorian architecture can still find some beautifully preserved examples on Carroll Avenue north of the Hollywood Freeway. Angel's Flight, the funicular railway that ran just one block, is gone. It used to be the cheapest train ride in the world—one cent. Gone too are the quaint swinging arm traffic signals that were once so much a part of the Los Angeles scene. Each time they changed, they went rrrr-ding, to alert daydreaming pedestrians audially as well as optically. Streetcars, both the yellow cars and the red, used to provide clean efficient transportation through the central city and to the suburbs. They still have their champions and may make a comeback in a modern form.

The Glamour Belt

"Hooray for Hollywood," sang Johnny "Scat" Davis back in the 1940s. It was impossible not to join the chorus and get caught up in the magic of that name. All the words ever written about Hollywood would probably circle the globe a couple of times. In fiction alone, more than 500 novels have a Hollywood setting. Hollywood is the greatest metaphor of the 20th century—in English and probably in as many other languages as films are shown in. If Hollywood can't claim to be the birthplace of the motion picture art, it was at least the nursery. Hollywood moviemakers have contributed dozens, possibly hundreds, of words to the language and given a new direction to at least one old word—glamour. Before movies, glamour attached only to royalty and nobility. No one else's activities counted for much. Hollywood put glamour within reach of former waitresses, typists, cab drivers, junk dealers and school dropouts. Further, the movie industry wrote the book on it for use by athletes, novelists, pilots, financiers, politicians, gangsters and just about anyone else worthy of news coverage. Becoming a movie actor was the quickest and most dazzling avenue of upward social mobility the world has ever known.

Hollywood, the place, as contrasted with Hollywood, the idea, is a child of Los Angeles, an adopted child, in fact. In the magnitude and rapidity of its change, the child has followed the parent's example. When it was first incorporated back in 1903, Hollywood was a religious and agricultural community of a few thousand souls. Less than twenty years later, having been annexed by Los Angeles, Hollywood had become the new Sybaris, the world's movie capital, with a population grown to 50 thousand. And a brief 25 years after that, the film capital was already looking back on its glorious past.

"How Hollywood has changed," must be the most frequently heard sentiment in town. It might have been said by the Calvinist citrus grower in 1920—and probably was. Or by the taxi driver of 1940, the hairdresser of 1950, the restaurateur of 1960, the disco operator of 1975. A photo of Hollywood Boulevard in the early 1900s shows an unpaved but neatly graded avenue with streetcar tracks running down its center. There are a few trees, fewer houses, and much farmland. Pure Norman Rockwell. Today the Boulevard is closer to a scene from Bosch or Bruegel, perhaps beyond them. It may just be the most colorful thoroughfare in the world.

(Preceding page) As the sun sets, the L.A. Basin begins to glow with its own lights, seen here from Mt. Wilson.

Hollywood, the name, survives as well as Hollywood, the place, even if only in few characteristic artifacts. It's enough, at least, to give heart to the sentimentalist. Take, for example, the anatomical memorials in cement at Grauman's Chinese Theater—except that it isn't Grauman's any more but Mann's. As a kind of logical extension to the Chinese Theater forecourt, a civic group has glamorized the sidewalks of Hollywood Boulevard with little pink stars, each honoring a film personality of past or present. Now, a past-president of the Bruce Cabot Fan Club can be assured that his old favorite will not be forgotten.

We can't visit Hollywood without taking a swing through Beverly Hills and ''the homes of the stars.'' A kind of medieval debate used to rage among social historians of the entertainment page whether this unique residential city, completely surrounded by the City of Los Angeles, was a suburb of Hollywood or whether in truth Hollywood was merely a satellite to Beverly Hills. Many of the stars have moved from Beverly Hills, but the extraordinary mansions remain for the most part. There's still plenty of glamour here.

In the 1920s, Beverly Hills successfully resisted annexation by the City of Los Angeles. Thirty years later the city fathers actually raised a monument to that struggle, a striking marble memorial, honoring Mary Pickford, Douglas Fairbanks, Will Rogers and other stars who led the fight for independence. Like the genesis of Hollywood itself, the flowering of Beverly Hills as the home of the stars was as brief as it was brilliant. In 1919 Douglas Fairbanks, Sr. was still hunting coyotes on the estate that was to become Pickfair. Since then, the great mansions of Summit Drive and the rest of the town were designed, built, lived in by legendary society, were handed on to less celebrated occupants, and in some cases fell to the wreckers ball; the more majestic the structure, the more vulnerable to removal. But the Beverly Hills Hotel survives and as long as it does, the faithful star-struck will have a symbol to look to as the British look to Gibraltar.

Immediately west of Beverly Hills is something new in glamour communities, Century City. It can't be without significance that in naming Century City the builders failed to specify which century. Built by ALCOA on 180 acres of the 20th Century Fox lot, Century City is a self-contained, complex of banks, office buildings, apartments, hotel and shopping center. The innovative Plaza Hotel was designed to be only two rooms wide so that every guest would have an outside view. Barely twenty-five years before ground was broken for Century City, the land it stands on

(Following page, above) Springtime brings colorful floral displays to Montana de Oro State Park, at Morro Bay.
(Following page, below) The Hollywood Freeway is in the foreground, Mt. Hollywood looms in the background in this view from Mulholland Drive.

was part of a ranch which had been a Spanish land grant. In some textbook of the future Century City may be cited as a blueprint for instant downtowns.

The residential splendor of Bel Air, Westwood, and Brentwood, reflects power and influence that has little to do with the entertainment world, although film people have lived in these communities. Here the glamour has its principal roots in banking, aerospace, oil, cattle, agriculture and publishing—''old money'' as reckoned by a Los Angeles calendar. This rock-solid, understated kind of glamour may be symbolized by the Los Angeles Country Club. Legend has it that actors have never been welcome to membership in the Club. Former western star Randolph Scott claims to have overcome the proscription by screening some of his old movies for the membership committee to prove that he was not an actor.

A singular monument in the Glamour Belt is Will Rogers State Historical Park, overlooking Pacific Palisades. The Park represents only about half of the original 350 acres of the cowboy philosopher's estate. The frame ranch house (now a museum) is modest and comfortable in a western style. It is in the space, the landscaping and the incredible view that the true luxury can be found. Below the house are the stables and polo field, one of the few such fields in the country. When it comes to luxury and glamour, it would be hard to top having your own polo field in the front yard.

(Preceding page, above) Looking as if it might fly itself, this building graces the L.A. International Airport complex.
(Preceding page, below) Sculptures dot the grounds of the L.A. County Museum of Art.

Tomorrowland Orange County

Twenty-five years ago the name Orange County would have produced neither smile nor frown of recognition at, say, a Boston or Chicago cocktail party. A few might have recollected a county in New York's Catskill Mountains or one on the Texas Gulf Coast. Today, in the minds of many Americans, Orange County is immediately associated with Southern California and Los Angeles. Among other things, it is likely to be recognized in business circles as the premier growth area in the country.

What produced the changed image? Unquestionably, a lot of social and economic forces have been at work; many, perhaps, too subtle for recognition. Among the more obvious are a massive shift in residence patterns in the Los Angeles Basin, the opening of the giant Irvine Ranch to development, and, not least, the advent of the greatest entertainment attraction of the century, Disneyland.

Orange was once part of Los Angeles County. In 1889 it broke away and had to look no further than the citrus groves around Fullerton and Santa Ana for a name. Not too long ago the County produced most of the nation's Valencias. That has changed. Between 1950 and 1965 a lot of orange trees had to give way to make room for the 11 new cities that were established in that period. Orange is already the second most populous county in California and on its way to becoming 800 square miles of what urbanologists now label ''urbanized space,'' too dense for a suburb, too dispersed for a city. Although the County has four cities of greater than 100 thousand, it lacks an urbanized core, a ''downtown.'' Many people who live there would like to keep it that way.

In 1950, when Jack Benny was still poking small-town fun at Anaheim, its population was less than 15,000. Only 20 years later it was 166,000. Today it is well over 200,000 and still climbing. So many businesses have moved to the County in this decade that sociologists are voicing serious fears of Los Angeles becoming the bedroom community. Most startling about the growth is that it is accompanied by an equally rapid rise in affluence. The decision of Nieman-Marcus to establish its first California store in Orange County can hardly be seen as whimsy.

(Following page, above) Montana de Oro State Park, Morro Bay offers a view of a rugged sea-land confrontation.
(Following page, below) A whimsical tower and bright floral display enliven this rocky section of coastline.

(Preceding page) Bright floral displays grace the grounds of Los Angeles City Hall.

(Opposite) Classic red-tile roofs grace the homes on the Palos Verdes peninsula, looking toward Redondo Beach.

(Right) Hibiscus come in a variety of colors, as most Los Angeles gardens will demonstrate.

(Below) The Huntington Gardens in San Marino provide peaceful vistas of classical statuary.

(Left) The Baldwin Hills offer this vista of Los Angeles' city center.

(Following page) This venerable three-master rides at anchor at Fishermen's Village, Marina del Rey.

(Second following page, above) Dolphins perform at Marineland, with a view of the blue Pacific in the background.

(Second following page, below) Buildings of the city seem to crowd close on this floral display in Pershing Square.

(Preceding pages) The view from the planetarium: spectacular sunset on one hand, city lights on the other.

(Left) Lovers of gardens and floral displays, Angelenos seem to create gardens wherever possible.

(Below) Modern Los Angeles architecture reaches for the sky, while leaving room for spacious malls between towers.

(Opposite) The lighthouse on Palos Verdes peninsula once warned ships of hazardous conditions.

(Following page) Red-tipped stalks of ocotillo grow in the desert near Blythe.

(Second following page, above) Houses stand close to a peaceful ocean at Malibu.

(Second following page, below) Banners decorate the plaza at University of Southern California's Von Kleinschmid Center.

(Opposite) Rows of palm trees line the Promenade at Palisade Park in Santa Monica.

(Right) Enjoying the virtually semi-tropical climate, hibiscus are popular with Los Angeles gardeners.

(Below) Wayfarer's Chapel, at Portuguese Bend, was designed by Frank Lloyd Wright.

(Following page, above) This daytime shot provides a look at the L.A. skyline from Baldwin Hills.

(Following page, below) The ornate Los Angeles Historical and Art Museum faces an extravagant rose garden.

There is at least a touch of irony in the fact that a community which appears headed into the future at jet speed should feature three tourist attractions most likely to draw visitors who are reaching back for a lost past—Disneyland, Knott's Berry Farm, and Lion Country Safari. To some extent all three purvey a nostalgia for things feared gone forever from American life—simple, unsophisticated family pleasures, a calm, unhurried society, a faith in hard work as the certain road to achievement. Disneyland, of the three, is the place most likely to turn the visitor nostalgic, which lends strength to the observation of Jack Smith and others that its principal appeal is to adults rather than children, that it plays back our myths. The Berry Farm is itself a black-ink witness to our folk conviction that through hard work and faith a roadside stand featuring homemade boysenberry jam and pie can be turned into a multi-million-dollar tourist attraction. The two Walts from Middle America, Knott and Disney, must have done their market research at the corner of Main and Elm.

Just what does tomorrow hold for this community which keeps at least one toe anchored cautiously in the past while it replaces orange groves with high-rise business complexes? With its unprecedented growth, its affluence and its new national identity, there is a question whether Orange County will be content to remain within the orbit of a Greater Los Angeles. In 1963, Orange County was first recognized by the U.S. Census Bureau as a metropolitan area distinct from Los Angeles under the impossibly awkward name of the Anaheim-Santa Ana-Garden Grove, California, Metropolitan Area. Increasingly these days residents of Fullerton, Buena Park, Anaheim, and other towns can be heard to identify themselves to non-Californians as coming from Orange County rather than using the town name. Not many years ago they probably would have told the host of a New York television talk show that they were from Los Angeles. As its urban area sweeps rapidly south toward the edge of Camp Pendleton, Orange County has it within its power to become an 800 square mile buffer city between Los Angeles and San Diego. It is acquiring some of the identifying marks of self-determination. It now has its own campus of the University of California, at Irvine. It has its own major league baseball team at Anaheim. But wait, here's evidence that old habits of mind die hard. After more than a decade of playing at Anaheim Stadium, Orange County's American League team is still called the Angels.

(Preceding page) Ports O' Call Village, near San Pedro harbor, strives for a quaint, Old World appearance.

The Rim of the Basin

Los Angeles Basin may be the most catch-all of catch-all expressions. It means vaguely the area between the mountains and the Pacific which more-or-less contains the City of Los Angeles and its neighbors. To get some sense of the size and complexity of the Basin from ground level and on a human scale, it's possible to drive around its perimeter, or most of it. Claremont is a good starting place, since it's close to the Los Angeles County line. Continue west on Foothill Boulevard through Glendora and the old San Gabriel Valley towns to Pasadena. At Pasadena we can switch to the Ventura Freeway, more typical of today's transit, drive through Glendale, a smidgen of Burbank, and on to the Laurel Canyon exit. Then south to Mulholland Drive, which for sentimental reasons is the most desirable route to the Coast Highway. That's roughly 90 miles without ever really being out of visual range of dense human settlement except toward the western end. The mileage figure alone gives some suggestion of the magnitude of "Supercity."

Anyone who has not driven Foothill Boulevard in a decade or so is likely to crane his neck in search of the citrus groves. They are gone, or nearly so. A land of private homes and shopping centers fills the scene to the south and west. With an occasional break—the Puente Hills, for example—this density of settlement may be imagined to stretch all the way to the ocean. On our right hand the urban tide is lapping at the San Gabriel Foothills. The inevitable question is how much further can we build in that direction? It feels as though right through the roof of the car the summit of Old Baldy is looming over our right shoulder. Will our grandchildren actually live in high-rise apartments atop Monrovia Peak? Before you say impossible, guess at the response of a Los Angeleno of 1879 if you could describe today's city to him.

Azusa, one of the old towns of the San Gabriel Valley citrus belt, is a name familiar to most middle-aged Americans, but for a curious reason. In the late 1940s, Azusa, along with Anaheim and Cucamonga, was the butt of a harmless running joke on the Jack Benny radio show. It soon became a national catchword. Azusa was born of the great land fever of the 1880s and its name conjures visions of that passionate belief in a golden future that seems so much a part of Southern California. Contrary to

(Following page, above) The J. Paul Getty Art Museum in Malibu is patterned after a Roman Villa.
(Following page, below) Evening sun sidelights the towers of city center, and traffic eases up on the Harbor Freeway.

legend, the town name does not derive from "everything from A to Z in the USA" though that folk etymology is marvelously revealing. Azusa seems to be an anglicized version of a Garieleno Indian name. As with so many towns in the Basin, it is difficult today to guess where Glendora, Duarte, and neighboring towns, end and Azusa begins. But thanks to its name, Azusa is not likely ever to lose its identity.

Arcadia's name, too, is familiar to people all over the country but for a very different reason; it is the home of the Santa Anita Racecourse. The declaration that Santa Anita is the world's most beautiful racetrack doesn't meet with much resistance among turf fans. Its light green grandstand and 500 acres of matchless landscape set against a backdrop of the San Gabriels would be hard to equal. Santa Anita first came to national prominence in the late 30s when, with the Depression not quite over, it ran the country's first $100,000 stake race. It was a spectacular instance of Los Angeles optimism.

Much of the land around Arcadia was part of the famous Rancho Santa Anita of the legendary mining tycoon, "Lucky" Baldwin. Some of the land now makes up the County and State Arboretum, an attraction no visitor should miss, especially if he has had a bad day at the track. Along with the Japanese Garden at San Marino, the Arboretum is one of the most peaceful places in the whole Basin. The serenity is not entirely attributable to the collection of exotic trees, plants, flowers and herbs, nor the songs of dozens of species of birds. The Arboretum is one of the few places in urban America that you can escape round-the-clock musical accompaniment: transistor radios and musical instruments are prohibited.

The next town along this route is a third familiar name, Pasadena. To most Americans Pasadena means the Tournament of Roses and the prototype of the now countless bowl games held in the Rose Bowl. Pasadena might more justly be known as a scientific and cultural center. Cal Tech is one of the giants of scientific education. The Jet Propulsion Lab makes Pasadena the dateline for news flashes of the space age. The Norton Simon Museum and, if we don't put too fine a point on city boundaries, the nearby Huntington Gallery and Library in San Marino draw many scholars.

Pasadena once boasted the highest per capita income of any city in America. The combination of its wealth, its superb setting in the Sierra Madre Foothills, and the almost total absence of industry may have represented at one time the highwater mark of suburban living in the world. Today's Pasadena is a lot more urbanized. The grand old mansions of Orange Grove Avenue now have to share the street with modern apartments. There are a lot of new buildings on Colorado Boulevard.

(Preceding page, above) The arches of Royce Hall frame UCLA's library.
(Preceding page, below) California poppies brighten this bluff above the beach at Montana de Oro State Park.

Actually, Pasadena has long been a bellwether of progress in the Basin. It was the first suburb to be served by the Pacific Electric at the turn of the century. It was also the first suburb to be connected with downtown by freeway. When the automobile has passed from the scene, Pasadena may be the first served by whatever the new form of transportation proves to be. But perhaps it's best not to think about such matters and just pick up the Ventura Freeway going west.

Glendale, rich in folktales of the late Casey Stengel, is the gateway to the San Fernando Valley, a triangular plain surrounded by mountains, which proved to be a real estate developers' Comstock Lode. Toward the end of World War II, Roy Rogers and the Sons of the Pioneers recorded a popular song whose refrain ended, "I'm going to settle down and never more roam/ And make the San Fernando Valley my home." More than a million Angelenos seemed to think that this made sense, and they followed suit. The Valley has become the largest single residential area of the City of Los Angeles, not counting the well-populated independent cities of Burbank and San Fernando. A couple of years ago a real estate developer took an aerial swing around the Valley and upon landing expressed astonishment at how much open land remained. If his observations were correct the Valley might eventually house more than half the City's population.

Mulholland Drive is forever woven into the romance of Los Angeles. Named for the engineer who masterminded the Owens Valley water project, which made modern Los Angeles possible, the highway winds through the Santa Monica Mountains and still offers some of the best vistas of both the City and the Valley, especially at night. In the 1930s Mulholland was a favorite haunt of young couples in jalopies—the Andy Hardy-Polly Benedict set—who wanted to neck while admiring the lights of the city below. That kind of low-key romantic activity may be but a memory. In any case, the police would almost surely advise against it. You can still admire the lights, even at 40 mph.

At Topanga Canyon the road becomes Mulholland Highway and corkscrews through some pretty country in the hills behind Malibu as it descends toward the ocean. This stretch is reminiscent of some old films, too, but not Andy Hardy. The automobile chase was a staple of pre-World War II movies and many a Buick touring car and Pierce Arrow was sent hurtling into the ravine to thrill Saturday afternoon audiences.

Our road finally connects with the Coast Highway at Leo Carrillo State Beach, a fitting place for the swing around the Basin to end. Leo Carrillo was an enormously popular character actor of the 30s and 40s, who specialized in heavily-accented

*(Left) A rose garden with an ocean view—
while in the background people enjoy the
sun and gentle surf at Laguna Beach.*

Hispanic roles. A native Angeleno, Carrillo was descended from one of the most prominent of the original Spanish families that settled the pueblo. His off-screen English was impeccable and unaccented. Perennially elected ''mayor'' of Encino, the personable Carrillo was never heard to raise a regretful protest against progress and the passing of the great ranchos of his ancestors. Significantly, he entered the business most responsible for transforming the image of Los Angeles, the motion picture industry. In true Angeleno style he jumped on the Hollywood bandwagon and rolled with enthusiasm towards an uncharted future.

The Blue Pacific
Malibu to Laguna

The Pacific Ocean is the largest, most spectacular natural feature on earth. Many of those who live by its shores also think it is the most beautiful. Los Angeles—a spectacular phenomenon in itself—can count among its blessings about a hundred miles of Pacific ocean front, much of it splendid pleasure beaches. Since the first Americans arrived in the Basin, these beaches have been a magnet for people seeking relaxation and beauty. Today, the supervised public beaches alone handle more than fifty million visitors a year, as nearly as can be estimated, and the term ''year round use'' may be taken literally. Even though the surf gets cool in the winter months, there are always a few hardy enthusiasts ready to brave it.

The busiest beaches are found in two strands—northern and southern—separated by Palos Verdes Peninsula, the most prominent feature of the coastline. Those to the north are properly the Los Angeles beaches. The beaches south of Long Beach are in Orange County. The northern group—Redondo, Hermosa, Manhattan, Venice, Santa Monica—have an aura of age that indicates how long visitors from nearby Los Angeles have been enjoying them. These northern beach towns are densely settled now; apartment complexes crowd close to the beach, where not many years ago there were scattered bungalows. A character from a Raymond Chandler novel, set in the L.A. of the 30s and 40s, might well lose his way. He would look in vain for the old familiar amusement park at Ocean Park, ''the Coney Island of the West.'' Gone, too, are the oil derricks, or they seem to be. In fact, there are still wells operating but they are covered by attractive structures that might be mistaken at first glance for small buildings.

Each of the old beach towns has its distinct and often colorful history dating to the era of land fever. Redondo Beach was once the object of so much speculative enthusiasm that individual land parcels were known to change hands as many as five times in a single day. Venice grew from the dream of Abbot Kinney, a wealthy and widely-traveled cigarette manufacturer. Enchanted on his visits to Italy by the queen of the Adriatic, Kinney decided to create Venice-by-the-Sea in Southern California. When completed, it boasted 16 miles of canal and an amusement park. Unfortunately, Kinney's canals raised some of the same problems as the canals in its

(Following page, above) This catamaran seems to be poised and waiting for a chance to go to sea.
(Following page, below) Fine homes are shaded under the pines and eucalyptus above San Pedro's harbor.

European model, stagnant water, garbage, insect pests, etc., and in time had to be filled in. An oil boom in Venice did further damage to Kinney's dreams. Today, little but archaeological evidence and some faded photos remain to remind us that residents once traveled the streets of the beach town in gondolas.

Malibu, charmingly walled against the sea by the surrounding Santa Monica Mountains, may be the most magical name among the beach towns. Like so many places in Los Angeles, Malibu acquired its initial fame from the presence of movie celebrities. Before automobiles were so plentiful, the remoteness of Malibu appealed to top stars, directors and producers as a refuge from publicity. There is a story that Irving Thalberg, the brilliant young producer at MGM, ordered his Malibu beach house soundproofed so that he would not be disturbed by the sound of the surf. Few have ever matched that grand gesture for conspicuous consumption. Of course, Malibu is more accessible today and much changed, but it is still charming. Houses have been built on the hillside and in the canyons. The seaside campus of Pepperdine University introduces an additional note of quiet dignity to what was once solely a resort community. Closer to the beach the exclusive Malibu Beach Colony survives comfortably and constitutes an attractive tie with the past.

Perhaps the most unusual house in Malibu is the J. Paul Getty Museum, a replica of a luxurious Roman villa. It is said that the oil man insisted upon reproducing a villa discovered in the ashes of Herculaneum, with its extensive porticos, reflecting pools, cypress trees and bronzes in the garden. He may have anticipated that his villa would not be well received by some scholars of architecture—and it hasn't been. But to the non-expert visiting the house and grounds, the villa feels and looks appropriate in Southern California's near-Mediterranean climate and landscape. More to the point, it makes an elegant setting for Getty's fine are collection. Getty was not born in Los Angeles, but he grew up there, in a large house on Wilshire Boulevard. When he was living in retirement in England, he used to talk fondly of the sunshine and playing in the surf as a boy. In a curious way, the Getty Museum may suggest an Angeleno impatience to get on with the business of growth, a desire to reach into the past for some instant ageing to apply to a city moving too fast to permit itself to mellow.

Like Athens, and Rome, who could not guess what they were destined to become, Los Angeles was established at a distance from the sea with little thought to the need for a harbor. And like the ancient cities, Los Angeles had to learn the hard way that history can force such issues. Facing a stretch of coast that lacks a natural

(Preceding page, above) This peaceful scene was captured at Descanso Gardens, La Canada.
(Preceding page, below) The campus of Pepperdine University overlooks the ocean at Malibu.

harbor, the city had to build one from scratch. It didn't get started until early in this century, and if railroadman Collis P. Huntington had had his wish the harbor would have been built at Santa Monica, an idea which today seems inconceivable. Huntington lost the debate and the harbor was built at San Pedro, the largest man-made harbor in the world.

The independent city of Long Beach, which shares the harbor with Los Angeles, is also one of the oldest seaside resorts. Generations of Navy men who served at Terminal Island have fond recollections of Long Beach and The Pike, the old amusement area. In the 1960s, in an admirably imaginative move to rejuvenate its tourist area, the City of Long Beach bought the retired Cunard Liner *Queen Mary* and berthed her at the mouth of the Los Angeles River. Refurbished and refitted with a tourist hotel, shops and marine exhibits, the broad-beamed *Queen* has grown into a top tourist attraction. The area around her berth has even been renamed Queen's Park. Saving the grand old ocean liner was a bold and gallant—and risky—gesture, but it was quite in the spirit of the region.

A visitor to busy, heavily-industrialized San Pedro might be surprised to learn that the western two-thirds of the Palos Verdes Peninsula is one of the most tranquil and rustic corners of the Los Angeles Basin. The hilly central portion of the peninsula is a country of handsome estates, white rail fences, paddocks, stables and miles of riding trails. But for the obvious differences in vegetation, a visitor might be fooled into thinking that he was in the horse country of Northern Virginia or Connecticut. A few country stores have even built hitching posts for their customers.

Lying just 23 miles off the coast of Palos Verdes is Santa Catalina Island, the best known of the Channel Islands and one of America's most unusual beauty spots. The wonderful old steamer, *S.S. Catalina*, no longer makes its unhurried daily cruises to Avalon, Catalina's only town, but five fast excursion boats do. You can catch one at San Pedro or Long Beach. If you are in a great hurry, you can even fly although why anyone would is hard to imagine. Catalina is a very tranquil place; its business is dispensing relaxation and quiet to visitors. Catalina's semitropical atmosphere has made it a favorite location for movies about "the South Seas." The island remains unspoiled largely through an accident of history. In 1919 chewing gum millionaire William Wrigley bought the whole island for three million dollars and decided to keep it pretty much as it is. A corporation set up by Wrigley maintains the island as an "unimproved" refuge for overheated and overworked Angelenos who need to escape for a recuperative weekend. Catalina even has its resident herd of buffalo, descendants of animals first brought to the island for the shooting of a Hollywood western.

(Following page) Sunset silhouettes the Music Center Fountain, with City Hall in the background.